LET THE EARTH BREATHE

GARDENING WITH NATIVE PLANTS

ANNE MILLIGAN
STEPHEN BROWN

ISBN: 978-0-9773158-7-1 (print)
ISBN: 978-0-9773158-1-9 (ePub)

TABLE OF CONTENTS

INTRODUCTION

Native Pink Muhly Grass (Muhlenbergia capillaris) at peak color in Louisville, Kentucky. October 16, 2021.

In the summer of 2009, my husband, Stephen Brown, and I prepared to leave our humble cottage in the woods (i.e., "employee housing") at the Abraham Lincoln Birthplace National Historic Park. Like displaced indigenous people of the rain forest, we wondered how we'd adjust to "city life" in our impending relocation to Louisville, Kentucky. One thing we knew: we could no longer live without trees. When we started looking for our next home, Steve had the idea to search on Google Earth for, of course, available properties next to some woods. That's how our journey began, creating a 12-plus years native botanical sanctuary at the edge of the woods in southeast Jefferson County, Kentucky. We are forever grateful to Margaret Shea at Dropseed Native Plant Nursery for her assistance in the beginning, and for providing such an amazing resource for native plants, shrubs, and trees in our area.

In this book, we hope to acquaint you with the following:

1. The fun and magic of biodiverse native gardening in Kentucky and its surrounding ecoregion within the United States. (Definition of biodiversity: *"Biological diversity in an environment as indicated by numbers of different species of plants and animals." (Merriam-Webster Dictionary)*
2. The reasons for choosing species native to your region (think pollinators) and some suggestions for species native to the Midwest and southeastern states, excluding Florida.
3. 100% immersion in the deep connections between species in nature, and your own connectedness to all of it.
4. Learning to slow down and practice patience by aligning with the growing cycles of various plant species and the associated role they play as hosts for a variety of caterpillars. For example, we have been waiting several years now for our young Pawpaw trees to bear fruit, and like good parents, we must let them find their own path to maturity. Meanwhile, we can provide them with an amenable environment in which to thrive while appreciating that, even when not fruiting, Pawpaws host the amazing Zebra Swallowtail Butterfly caterpillar. We had our first Pawpaw fruits in 2019, and we can emphatically say they are delicious and worth the wait!
5. Native plant lists and suggestions on how to site plants, shrubs and trees according to a variety of conditions such as sun/shade, soil moisture requirements; and height, color, and bloom times.
6. Landscaping ideas for the home garden that appeal to the esthetics of beauty, shape, and form that are appropriate for many neighborhoods and HOA expectations.
7. Seed swaps and sharing native plants, shrubs, and trees with neighbors and friends. If everyone who owns property would remove at least one exotic species and replace it with a native species, this would make a remarkable difference for pollinators and for the earth. Our dream is to help the earth breathe more freely.
8. One dollar from the sale of each book goes to the "Let The Earth Breathe" nonprofit organization for restoring native habitat. http://lettheearthbreathe.org/

We hope this book adds inspiration for many others to plant natives. The health of our planet lies in the health of our pollinators and their host trees, shrubs, and plants. Let the earth breathe!

Stephen Brown and Anne Milligan
2021

HERE IS A TEMPLATE TO HELP YOU PLAN YOUR NATIVE GARDEN

As you go through this book, you can use this chart to note which plants you like best, and research more about their qualities. See the Appendix for plant lists.

Plant	Full Sun	Shade	Part Sun & Shade	Bloom Time	Blossom Color	Height	Soil Preference: wet/dry/both

WHY BIODIVERSITY AND WHY NATIVE PLANTS?

"We need biodiversity because biodiversity runs the ecosystem on which we depend. The more diverse an ecosystem is, the more services (air, water, food, benign weather systems, carbon dioxide sequestration, garbage recycling, etc.), it will provide for us."

— Douglas Tallamy, author of the book "Bringing Nature Home."

Native plant species are better than exotic non-natives for the following reasons:

- Biodiversity adds variety to a bland diet, like an infant being introduced to solid food after a steady diet of strained beets and carrots. Nothing against beets or carrots (Steve prefers pizza).
- We still think grass is okay in small doses, but native plants offer so much more variety, with vibrant blossoms in every conceivable color.
- Native plants attract a variety of birds, butterflies, and other wildlife by providing diverse habitats and food sources. Closely mown lawns and exotic ornamental plants and shrubs are of little use to most wildlife and pollinators.
- Native plants help us use less water.
- Native species are usually perennials: they return every year, saving time and money spent on annuals. Planting a variety of native perennials that bloom at different times of the growing season provides years of multi-season enjoyment for humans, and especially for bees, butterflies, birds, and all pollinators.

Some people dream of diamonds and riches. Not me. I dream of the restoration of tall native prairie grasses, native wildflowers, and the return of the prairie birds, bees, and butterflies. I dream of food forests, organic vegetable gardens, and neighbors with chickens, ducks, and rescue critters of all kinds, including senior dogs who come to just hang out in the shade and stay warm in the winter. I dream of the end, finally, of our addiction to "lawn care." I don't want mechanical, low, droning sounds penetrating our peaceful spaces. I dream of the sounds of bird calls, the wind in the trees, and the buzzing of bumblebees shaking the life source out of their flowers. I want human beings to fall in love with the vast array of color that gives spice, soul, and curious interest to our coexistence on the planet. And I want every living thing on earth to recognize the highest value and purpose for itself.

—Anne Milligan

A rain garden with Orange Coneflower (*Rudbeckia fulgida*), Cardinal Flower (*Lobelia Cardinalis*), Seedbox (*Ludwigia alternifolia*), Swamp Hibiscus (*Hibiscus Moscheutos*), and Joe Pye Weed (*Eupatorium Fistulosum*.) A Pawpaw tree (*Asimina Triloba*) is at the back edge.

INVASIVE EXOTICS VERSUS NATIVE PLANTS

From our experiences, we learned that exotic ornamental plants may be pretty for human beings but offer very little or nothing for pollinators.

Japanese Honeysuckle, for example, is considered an invasive species because it forms dense root structures that prevent neighboring plants and seeds from reaching the soil.

In the before and after photos, compare the barren ground, where only Japanese Honeysuckle can grow, with the beautiful native plant species growing in harmony with each other.

Common Non-Native Invasive Species	Suggested Native Alternatives
Privet	Red Chokeberry, Ninebark, American Holly
Burning Bush	Eastern Wahoo, Black Chokeberry, Winterberry Holly
Tree of Heaven	Serviceberry or Kentucky Coffee Tree
Bradford Pear/Callery Pear Tree	American Plum, Serviceberry, Eastern Redbud, or Yellowwood Tree
Japanese Honeysuckle	Coral Honeysuckle (*Lonicera Sempervirens*)
Pampas Grass	Pink Muhly Grass, Big Bluestem
Multiflora Rose	Carolina Rose
Mimosa Tree	Fringe Tree or Red Buckeye
Princess Tree	Native Dogwoods, Catalpa Tree
English Ivy	Crossvine, Coral Honeysuckle, Allegheny Spurge
Butterfly Bush	Fragrant Sumac
Japanese Barberry	Virginia Sweetspire, Arrowwood Viburnum, Black Chokeberry, Red Chokeberry
Nandina domestica	American Holly, St. John's Wort, Ninebark, Northern Hackberry, common Hop tree
Golden Bamboo	River Cane (*Arundinaria gigantea*), Wild Ginger, Groundsel, Sundrops, Violets, Pennsylvania Sedge, Blazing Star
Invasive Wintercreeper (*Euonymus fortunei*)	Wild Ginger, Groundsel, Sundrops, Violets, Pennsylvania Sedge
Purple Loosestrife	Blazing Star
Tall Fescue Grass	Pennsylvania Sedge, Blue-Eyed Grass, Cherokee Sedge, Muhly Grass

From Garden to *"Yarden"*

Creating a home "yarden" landscape (converting most of your yard into a garden) with a biodiverse collection of native plants, shrubs, and trees is good for the environment, plus it offers a stunning array of possibilities for year-round color, texture, and flow. We feel deprived when we visit wild places that have been untended and taken over by invasive species such as Privet, Kudzu, Japanese Honeysuckle, and Multiflora Rose. These places often have little else growing around the invasive plants and the whole area appears barren.

Dr. Douglas Tallamy, author of the book "Bringing Nature Home," lists species which are hosts for the *largest* numbers of moth and butterfly larvae in the United States. It is highly recommended that gardeners focus on these species first in planning native landscapes. Below, we provide some of the species that are suggested by Tallamy, and then some of the Kentucky/Midwestern natives.

Quercus (Oak)	Black Oak - *Quercus velutina* Bur Oak - *Quercus macrocarpa* Chestnut Oak - *Quercus prinus* Chinkapin Oak - *Quercus muehlenbergii* Northern Red Oak - *Quercus rubra* Pin Oak - *Quercus palustris* Scarlet Oak - *Quercus coccinea* Shingle Oak - *Quercus imbricaria* *White Oak - Quercus alba* *Willow Oak - Quercus phellos*
Salix (Willow)	Pussy Willow – *Salix discolor*
Prunus (Cherry)	Black Cherry - *Prunus serotina*
Pinus (Pine)	Eastern White Pine - *Pinus strobus* Virginia Pine - *Pinus virginiana* Loblolly Pine - *Pinus taeda L.*
Betula (Birch)	River Birch - *Betula nigra* Sweet Birch - *Betula lenta*
Vaccinium (Blueberry)	Northern highbush blueberry -*Vaccinium corymbosum*
Acer (Maple)	Red Maple - *Acer rubrum* Sugar Maple - *Acer saccharum*
Carya (Hickory)	Pignut Hickory - *Carya glabra* Shagbark Hickory - *Carya ovata* Shellbark Hickory - *Carya laciniosa*
Malus (Crabapple)	Southern Crabapple - *Malus angustifolia*
Ulmus (Elm)	American elm - *Ulmus americana* Slippery elm - *Ulmus rubra* Winged elm - *Ulmus alata* Rock elm - *Ulmus thomasii*
Tillia (Basswood)	American Linden - *Tilia americana*
Crattaegous (Hawthorne)	Cockspur Hawthorn - *Crataegus crus-galli* Green Hawthorn - *Crataegus viridis*
Fraxinus (Ash Trees)	*Green Ash – Fraxinus pennsylvanica* Blue Ash - *Fraxinus quadrangulata*

IN FAVOR OF BIODIVERSITY IN HOME GARDENS

The primary problem with exotic/invasive species is that they often crowd out any other species but their own. Left unchecked, this creates a "monoculture" which is NOT part of a healthy, biodiverse, ecosystem. Plus, it's boring to look at.

(Above) Orange Coneflower, Great Blue Lobelia, Echinacea, Cardinal Flower, and Blue Flag Iris. (R) Joe Pye Weed, Bee Balm, Indigo Bush, Swamp Milkweed, Illinois Bundleflower, Carolina Rose, Purple Coneflower, Seedbox, Cut-leaf Prairie Dock, Coral Honeysuckle . . . and unexpected guests, pictured below.

Purple coneflower (*Echinacea*) with a Great Spangled Fritillary.

YEAR ONE: 2010

Creating a Biodiverse Landscape from an Ordinary Yard

DIGGING OUR FIRST RAIN GARDEN IN 2010

Steve: I learned a lot more about poison ivy than I had planned for when we started clearing the invasive Japanese honeysuckle that was encroaching on a small barren spot next to our house. A dense mat of fibrous roots overwhelmed the rototiller, stopping the tines in less than a minute, yet the roots were no match for the native Jewel Weed seeds that had been lying dormant beneath the impenetrable layer. When we added organic material to the clearing, the Jewel Weed sprang back to life and we had orange, trumpet-shaped blossoms growing that first summer before we knew what they were. It was almost like Mother Nature had rewarded our efforts by extending a welcome mat of native flowers. It wasn't long until Mist Flower, Tickseed, Coreopsis, and many more native varieties, joined them.

Anne: I recall the blank spot on the ground where the previous owners of our new property had parked their boat. Not willing to allow the Japanese honeysuckle to retake that spot, we set about doing something with it that was aligned with our intention to create a native plants habitat. As embarrassing as it is to admit, we didn't even have a wheelbarrow when we decided to tackle the tons of gravel which came with the landscaping. Consequently, we spent the first year moving the gravel in buckets. (Keep an eye out for the "blue bucket" in the photos.)

Here is a small sample of the native plants currently thriving in a once-barren space:

- Cardinal Flower
- Great Blue Lobelia
- Echinacea (Purple Coneflower)
- Orange Coneflower
- Tall Tickseed
- Joe Pye Weed
- Obedient Plant
- Meadow Phlox

Koi Pond to Fern Garden

Anne: March 2010, Steve and I were staring at the koi pond that came with the house and yard. When the previous owners told us that a heron kept eating the koi, we started secretly cheering for the heron.

Steve: Our prayers were answered. The heron ate the rest of the koi—a non-native species. We pulled the black plastic liner out of the first pond and discovered four feet of sludge.

Encouraged, we removed the other liner and offered them for sale online.

Ferns are survivors, dating from the Mesozoic Age, making them an ideal "black-thumbed" gardener's choice for shady areas.

(Below) That is a Royal Fern in the shallow water, with its tall fronds just starting to unfurl. It helps to talk to the plants. The Cinnamon Fern at the lower right has been listening to Steve . . . "Grow, or you're history, buddy!"

We sought guidance from botanist Margaret Shea of Dropseed Nursery because we didn't know what to do with this muddy hole in the ground. Margaret suggested that we fill the hole with organic materials such as leaves, hay, and manure from the elephant house at the Louisville Zoo, etc. So that's what we did, and the ferns have been thriving for at least 12 years with no help from us except the addition of a handful of lime powder once a year.

Same hole—one year later in 2011—after adding native ferns, dirt, leaves, some water, and letting the Sun and Earth do the rest. There are no "Green-thumbed" or "Black-thumbed" gardeners—although hardy native plants improve the odds for positive results.

And the same fern bog in 2019:
Royal, Lady, Sensitive, and Maidenhair Ferns

More About Ferns…

Southern Maidenhair Ferns have a root structure that is easily divided and transplanted, making them perfect for filling out shady areas. And they make a beautiful border for mostly-shaded walkways. Royal Ferns, below left, are fascinating to watch as they unfurl their fronds when Spring arrives.

LEARNING ABOUT OTHER NATIVE PLANTS FOR MOIST SOILS

2010 placement of our first Kentucky native plants. In planning this garden, we chose plants according to the site conditions: 1. Partial sun; 2. Heavy clay soil; 3. Expected height of the plants: (Taller plants toward the back); 4. Plants that can handle seasonally moist to flooded soil. Water from the roof drained down the center of this site, so we dug a channel for the water to meander through the garden and exit at the lowest spot where it would eventually flow into the next rain garden.

(2012) My, how quickly they fill out!

In this garden:

Cardinal Flower;

Great Blue Lobelia;

Black-Eyed Susan;

Joe Pye;

Seedbox;

Monkey Flower;

Purple Coneflower;

Mistflower.

Plants don't "die," they participate in the organic life cycle. There is no reason to fear gardening failure.

Note the eggshells and coffee grounds from our compost pile.

The photo on the left shows a beautiful shady woodland native called "Cardinal Flower" (*Lobelia cardinalis*).

Great Blue Lobelia (*Lobelia Siphilitica*) is also a beautiful shady woodland native that, like Cardinal Flower, is a hummingbird magnet.

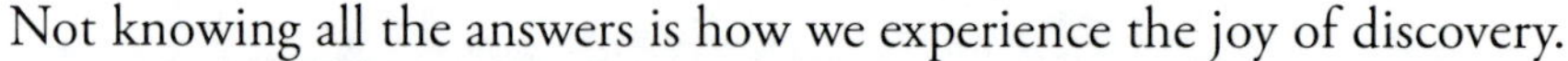

2010: "WHAT IN THE HECK ARE WE DOING?"

Not knowing all the answers is how we experience the joy of discovery.

SOME ASSISTANCE FROM A WATER FAIRY

There was a time (pictured above) when we looked at each other and thought, "What in the living heck are we DOING?" We didn't know much about rain gardens, other than attending a single, one-day class. However, we were aware that the landscape had a gradual slope away from the house, and that, in a heavy rain, the water quickly filled up the first rain garden and flowed downhill to the open field that abuts our back yard. We had ALMOST made the decision to dig the rain garden such that it flowed straight back, like a ditch (see photo). That was not to be, however, for that night Anne was visited in a dream by a female figure lovingly called the "water fairy." She was quite emphatic that the flow of the first rain garden should NOT flow straight back like a residential ditch, but, rather, should flow down diagonally across the backyard. So, of course, we dug the rain garden diagonally across the back yard. It has turned out beautifully because that flow inspired two more rain gardens that connect one to the other until the water flows out the far corner of the yard to another drainage going downhill.

Moral of the Story: Listen to the Water Fairies!

Rain gardens capture stormwater runoff and help keep water clean by filtering it before it reaches local streams. This helps alleviate flooding and drainage problems, helps replenish the ground water supply, and enhances beauty while supporting biodiversity by attracting birds and butterflies.

The original plan of channeling water off the roof into a rain garden has expanded. (And improved!) Since a light, five-minute rain will fill a 55-gallon barrel, we connected two barrels to serve as a reservoir. The system worked so well, we installed rain barrels at the opposite corner in the front of the house and installed another rain garden.

UNEXPECTED DELIGHTS

Mother Nature is a whimsical opera buff, a tree frog the size of my thumb is cast as a Basso Profundo, the lowest operatic role. I can't see them, so the crickets must be in the orchestra pit on percussion. A song bird trills an aria. A grackle is typecast as the villain; his raucous caw a harbinger of malicious intent. A squirrel perched in the tree screeches like a critic. Intermission.

—Stephen Brown

(Below) A goldfinch gathers seeds. A ladybug takes a siesta; a Monarch Butterfly caterpillar feasts on milkweed, and our typecast grackles take a bath.

Orange coneflower (*Rudbecia fulgida*) and Great blue lobelia (*Lobelia siphilitica*)

YEAR TWO: 2011

Creating the Second Rain Garden

2011: Steve began loosening and amending the hard-packed heavy clay soil with peat moss and compost/humus for our second rain garden. Mosquitos need standing water for 7 days in order for larvae to hatch. By mixing in soil amendments two feet deep, the rain water soaks into the ground before mosquitos have time to breed! And, just like in our first rain garden, there is an exit for water to flow out and downhill to the next rain garden in our landscape. We created the berm to hold the water a while longer, thus keeping it out of city drainage systems and naturally filtering out impurities. (As the plants matured, our first rain garden has naturally evolved to be almost as good at absorbing vast amounts of rainwater.)

Same rain garden a few years later. The task before us is a portal to the beauty around us. The Indigo bush partially obscuring Steve is the same one in the pot in the above picture.

WITNESSING THE MIRACLE OF METAMORPHOSIS

A female Monarch butterfly lays her eggs on Milkweed plants and nothing else, so we always include various types of Milkweeds native to the region. A migrating Monarch butterfly deposited her eggs on a Swamp Milkweed leaf. A caterpillar emerged and feasted on the leaves. It doubled in size every couple of days, and when it was ready, it crawled to a nearby Maximillian's Sunflower. With a spot of self-made glue, it attached itself to the bottom of a leaf, curled itself into a "J" shape, and spun a dark green chrysalis. We waited and waited, checking it every day to see if anything new happened. When the chrysalis became transparent, we knew something BIG was getting ready to happen. And oh, the amazing moment when the egg-to-butterfly cycle was complete as it freed itself from the outer shell and flew away.

Milkweeds for the Midwest

1. Common Milkweed (*Ascelpias syriaca*)
2. Orange Milkweed (*Asclepias tuberosa*)
3. Rose (or "Swamp") Milkweed (*Asclepias incarnata*)
4. Honeyvine (*Cynanchum laeve*) [Weedy, but in the milkweed family]
5. Aquatic Milkweed (*Asclepias Perennis*)

Many native plants are butterfly magnets and larval hosts. Spicebush Swallow Tail Butterfly on Cardinal flower (*Lobelia cardinalis*)

YEAR THREE: 2012

The Third Rain Garden and Learning to Slow Down

WE ARE REWARDED WITH MANY NEW VISITORS

Maybe we don't need to hurry. This is the snail who cleans our fern garden fountain when the birds aren't lining up at bath time.

Bee Balm (Monarda) attracts so many bumblebees, we hear them buzzing before we see them. Bee Balm is also very popular with butterflies who feed from the nectar. Added bonus: (R) the Clearwing Moth

IN FAVOR OF NATIVE SHRUBS

Chokeberry shrubs are early bloomers and a welcome sign that Spring is here to stay. When the blossoms have faded, the fruit has ripened, and the leaves are but a memory, the deep purple berries on a Chokeberry (below left) often remain into winter. These colorful berries taste so tart, they are a starving bird's meal-of-last-resort, nature's way of ensuring that local birds have something to eat when they grow truly desperate. When the last Chokeberry berries are "choked-down," the first fruits of Spring are but a short hunger-strike away. (Bottom center) Spice bush is another early bloomer in March! (Bottom Right) Elderberry blooming in May.

A Native Shrubs List:

- Chokeberry (*Aronia melanocarpa*)
- Ninebark (*Physocarpus opulifolius*)
- Elderberry (*Sambucus nigra*)
- Shrubby St. John's Wort (*Hypericum prolificum*)
- Jewelweed (*Impatiens campensis*)
- Arrowwood Viburnum (*Viburnum dentatum*)
- Spicebush (*Lindera benzoin*)
- Snowberry (*Symphoricarpos albus*)
- Coralberry (*Symphoricarpos orbiculatus*)
- Carolina Rose (*Rosa Carolina*)
- Fragrant Sumac (*Rhus aromatica*)
- Winterberry (*Ilex verticillate*)
- Red-Twig Dogwood (*Cornus sericea*)
- Carolina Allspice (*Calycanthus floridus*)

THE CREATION OF OUR THIRD RAIN GARDEN IN 2012

All of our rain gardens flow slightly downhill, away from the house. In a heavy rain, they can fill up fast, and flow out of the exits we created. Our intention is to hold the rainwater long enough for some of it to sink down into the water table. The native plants in the rain gardens clean the water and nourish the soil. Rain Gardens do tend to evolve year over year, as native plants create their own ecosystem. As you might guess by now, rainwater meanders into this rain garden #3 from the overflow of Rain Garden #2

Anne amended the heavy clay soil with a mixture of peat moss and humus manure in order to ensure that rain water drains down into the water table below, thus keeping mosquitos from breeding in standing water.

I (Anne) created this rain garden as a natural way for rain water to flow from the second rain garden down into this one in heavy rains. I worked on it by myself in a time when my career as a psychotherapist was coming to an end due to overwhelming burnout. It truly kept me from becoming physically ill from the stress of too much caring. I'm convinced that, for anyone in any stressful situation, gardening is therapeutic for body, mind, and spirit.

RAIN GARDEN #3 TWO YEARS LATER

Southern Blue Flag Iris thrives in lightly flooded areas.

Bumblebees follow the yellow "guide" down into the tunnel of the Blue Flag Iris blossom, and when they back out of the tunnel, they have pollen on their backs, which they transfer to the nearby flowers, thus participating in Earth's wonderful gift of pollination.

NOTE: A few years into our project, a friend gifted us with a clump of beautiful, but non-native, cream-colored Irises. Every year, we notice the gorgeous flowers, but the bees have absolutely nothing to do with them. This iris species has not evolved along with the native bees, so they are ornamental, and for humans, only. We find ourselves less and less interested in purely ornamental plants because they lack any of the vitality we see in the fluttering of a wide variety of butterflies, bees, and moths around the native species. The same could be said for the truly beautiful Tulip varieties from Holland. We still grow those in planter boxes, but I (Anne) always feel a little sad because nothing in the pollinator world pays any attention to them, making them essentially barren.

OTHER NATIVE SPECIES THAT FOUND THEIR WAY TO RAIN GARDEN #3 AND STAYED!

By the summer of 2020, we were surprised to see that some natives that do perfectly fine in dry prairie gardens also don't mind the seasonal flooding of a sunny rain garden. One of those is a lovely legume plant called "Illinois Bundleflower" (*Desmanthus illinoensis*). Also growing in this rain garden is Swamp Hibiscus, Orange Coneflower, Buttonbush, Blue Flag Iris, and Elderberry (along the edges).

SPEAKING OF LEGUMES...

Native legumes are part of a wonderful family of plants that actually fertilize the soil in which they grow, making it more amenable for other plants to grow alongside them. That is quite a different "attitude" than the tendency of some invasive, non-native plants to PREVENT other species from growing around them. Here is a list of some of the more common, and accessible, native legume species for Kentucky and the Midwestern states:

Illinois Bundleflower (*Desmanthus illinoensis*)

American Senna (*Senna hebecarpa*)

Indigo Bush (*Amorpha fruticose*)

Eastern Redbud Tree (*Cercis canadensis*)

Partridge Pea (*Cassia fasciculata*)

Purple Prairie Clover (*Dalea purpurea*)

White Prairie Clover (*Dalea candida*)

Blue False Indigo (*Baptisia Australis*)

(R) Showy Tick Trefoil (*Desmodium canadense*)

YEAR FOUR: 2013

We find somewhere to sit down and rest

Creating a native plants sanctuary was so labor-intensive in the first three years, that by 2012, we realized that we didn't even have a place to sit. We began to spend a little more time watching and waiting. That's when the magic began. We noticed how pollinators preferred certain host plants on which to lay their eggs. And we delighted in new pollinators, drawn to our gardens by specific native plants.

Taking a break in the middle of another muddy project. (Sitting!)

Still working out the water flow from one rain garden to the next.

Note the French drain that Steve installed to channel rain water from a roof pipe to the rain garden.

Plants grow better with rain water because rain contains nitrogen, which is immediately taken up by the roots and leaves of our native plants. Also, rain water doesn't carry the chemicals used to purify drinking water.

ADDICTED TO LAWN CARE

Have I got a deal for you: Spend more money. Work extra, so there is more work to do. Repeat on a weekly basis. Can you imagine someone coming to your door and trying to sell you on this plan?

This is what modern lawn care is promising—and delivering. Spending money on fertilizer and other chemicals that are harmful to the environment, in order to make the grass grow faster, so I have to cut it more often. No thanks. I'd rather spend lawn-care money on something that's fun and enjoy our garden. This is the view from where I'm sitting instead of mowing. And close-ups of a couple visitors.

MARCH—THE MONTH OF "ANYTHING GOES"

It was snowing large clumps of wet snow in late March 2013, and yet signs of spring were everywhere. One of the many reasons we love being surrounded by native perennials is that these plants are hardy; they return every year from the roots and seeds, and they keep going no matter what the weather does. Native plants have adapted to the seasons—long before we came here—and will continue to do so long after we're gone.

My respect for these plants grows with each season, I bow before this kind of endurance and am humbled and inspired by their resilience. I'm training my inner Self to endure, to be patient, to be consistently at peace and focused on my purpose for being here, no matter the storms outside—I don't want to be moved every time a troll appears, intent on destruction and unbalancing. I don't want to react; I want to act, and I want to do so deliberately, intentionally, and out of an internal environment of peace and self-respect. In doing so, I attract respect, kindness, goodness, and peaceful energy in people.

It's a beautiful thing, this being alive business. What is placed before us is a choice: the blessing or the curse, life or death. WE choose. Each individual chooses. I'm choosing life, and one of the most fun and effective ways to give life is to garden with native plants and then share in the harvest with others.

CORAL HONEYSUCKLE

(*Lonicera Sempervirens*) Blooms in May, July, *and* September

First sign of Coral Honeysuckle leaves returning, in late February, 2013.

Coral Honeysuckle partially open and in full bloom in late May.

The American Indian Cherokee tribe used May Apples to treat constipation, earaches, warts, and deafness. The local deer certainly appear healthy, since they harvest the fruit before we get a chance to test the efficacy.

Pollinators on the following (Clockwise):
Rose Milkweed,
Passion Flower,
Monkey Flower,
Joe Pye Weed.

UNEXPECTED SIGHTINGS ARE A BUG BONUS!

With so much attention placed on the survival of Monarch butterflies and honeybees, we may sometimes forget that there are a huge number of other insects which function as pollinators and food sources for animals that inhabit our ecosystems. With the evolution of our growing native plants sanctuary, we have been delighted to discover so many new insects! For example, did you know that honeybees are not native to our continent? However, there are approximately 4,000 native bee species that are declining because of habitat loss. As homeowners, they depend on us to plant the species they need and to keep our "yardens" as natural as possible for their wintering over. This can include ***leaving the leaves****.

* **Leaving the Leaves:** We learned that many caterpillars pupate in leaf litter, so we do not want to destroy their overwintering sites. We want all of the pollinators to thrive, which is why we're doing all of this in the first place. Now, since we don't have much grass left anyway, we most definitely "leave the leaves" where they fall. We have noticed an increase in skippers, butterflies, and specialty bees.

BIRDS, BIRDS, BIRDS!

One of the wonderful things about a native plants project is observing the natural cycles on an annual basis. One of those cycles is the return of certain birds, since they have connections to native plants and shrubs, via fruits and seeds. As we expand the diversity of native plants, shrubs, and trees, we see more wildlife of all kinds. Here is a small sample of what we see each season:

Early Spring: Robins and Cardinals begin constructing nests in the thick brambles of Coral Honeysuckle.

Mid to late Spring: Cardinals relish the red berries from the first crop of Coral Honeysuckle blossoms. Hummingbirds return, feeding extensively from the blossoms of Coral Honeysuckle and later, Cardinal Flower, and Great Blue Lobelia, etc.

Summer: Goldfinch come for the seeds of native Echinacea in order to feed their young. Blue jays love blackberries and Robins get as many ripe blueberries as they can stuff in their mouths. Cedar Waxwings absolutely love ripe Elderberries.

Fall: Many varieties of birds come in late summer for the fruits of Spicebush, Coral Honeysuckle, Chokeberry, Viburnum, etc.

Winter: Year-round birds feast on seeds from native plants, grasses, and sedges. We don't need to buy packages of bird seed.

Hummingbird Nectar Native Plants

Coral Honeysuckle: (*Lonicera sempervirens*)
Cardinal Flower (*Lobelia cardinalis*)
Great Blue Lobelia (*Lobelia siphilitica*)
Jewelweed (*Impatiens capensis*)
Lavender & Scarlet Bee Balms (*Monarda*)
Columbine (*Aquilegia canadensis*)
Beardtongue (*Penstemon digitalis*)
Crossvine (*Bignonia capreolata*)
Royal Catchfly (*Silene regia*)
Red Buckeye (*Aesculus pavia*)

ELDERBERRY BUSH: A VERY EASY SHRUB FOR NEW GARDENERS

Elderberry bushes are almost impossible to kill—even better, easy to root. Steve accidently broke off a branch, stuck it in the ground, and the next year it bore fruit.

Warning: birds and wives are equally fond of the berries.

(Anne): I can verify that. The purple-black berries are very tasty when fully ripe!

(Below) Elderberry fruit (droops) and a blossom.

LEARNING ABOUT NATIVE SEDGES

Photos: Cherokee Sedge (*Carex Cherokeensis*):
What a difference two years makes. Native plants come back bigger and stronger every year.

As mentioned previously, we created our rain garden system to collect water from the roof, and so we have quite a lot of water running through our extended garden in a heavy rain. We deliberately designed the rain gardens to temporarily hold the water long enough to allow it to sink into the water table, and then flow out of the rain gardens and into an easement that abuts our back yard.

Along the way, we discovered certain hardy plants called "sedges" that don't mind growing alongside, and sometimes right in the middle of, the shallow drainages. Sedges can be used to prevent erosion on slopes. Some other types of native sedges actually grow in dry shade. Sedges provide shelter for small animals, and seeds for birds and turtles. Many sedges also support the caterpillar stage of butterflies, moths, and skippers.

Here are some native sedges that are currently thriving in our rain gardens:

Fox Sedge (*Carex Vulpinoidea*)

Frank's Sedge (*Carex Frankii*)

Cherokee Sedge (*Carex Cherokeensis*)

Outside the rain gardens, in dry woodland areas, we have planted the following:

Appalachian Sedge (*Carex Appalachia*)

Pennsylvania Sedge (*Carex Pennsylvanica*)

SPICEBUSH AND PAWPAW

Spicebush is a lovely native shrub with edible red berries. It is a host plant for the Spicebush Swallowtail butterfly caterpillar. Spicebush is one of the first woodland shrubs to blossom in early Spring.

Pawpaw trees are host plants for Zebra Swallowtail butterflies—notice the zebra-like stripes on the caterpillar. Pawpaw blossoms smell like rotten meat to attract the carrion bugs who are their natural pollinators. The diversity is fascinating, the fruit—a tropical delight.

Directly participating in the nurturing of native plants brings so many surprises & some interesting ways that we can learn about ourselves, if we're open. This is a Pawpaw seedling pushing its way out of a thick seed coating. Notice how strong the trunk is already. The roots have been growing much longer than the leaves that are pushing out of the seed husk. This is a seed from the very first native plants and seeds swap that we put together in the Louisville, Kentucky area via our Facebook group. We consider this a sign that our work will continue, despite many obstacles, and the benefits will grow exponentially as more people learn about home gardening landscapes with native plants, shrubs and trees.

Eventually, the above-mentioned Pawpaw was ready to fully release itself from the seed casing and it has been growing by leaps and bounds ever since!!

BUTTERFLIES AND MOTHS ARE REGULAR VISITORS TO NATIVE PLANTS

Clockwise from upper left:
Tiger Swallowtail,
Dark Morph Tiger Swallowtail,
Great Spangled Fritillary,
Luna Moth,
Painted Lady,
and another Eastern Tiger Swallowtail with luminescent blue markings.

MORE VISITORS!

Adding a water feature to the garden creates tranquil resting spots and draws songbirds and other unexpected visitors.

A COUPLE MORE VISITORS

JULY: WHEN EVERY DAY IN THE GARDEN IS A DELIGHT

It's hard to believe this was once all grass. In this scene, every plant is native to Kentucky and the surrounding region, including Anne!

Below: In mid-August, other native species begin to bloom: Great Blue Lobelia, Joe Pye Weed, Cardinal Flower, and Orange Coneflower.

Interactive Colors of Native Wildflower Blossoms:

"It is so enjoyable to see the intense "WOW" colors of individual native wildflower blossoms, but it is the interactions of certain colors that add spice and wonder to our gardens. Sometimes, these interactive colors happen on their own, but we can also design them intentionally, thus adding another level of pizzazz to a garden area. In this photo, for example, we see that the radiant violet purple of native Ironweed (*Veronia gigantea*) is even more intense as seen against the bright (complementary) color of Orange coneflower. On a color wheel (which one can purchase at any art store or online), you can find a color, and its opposite (complementary) color and plant native wildflowers that bloom at the same time in those colors. Another example is Cardinal Flower (*Lobelia cardinalis*). Its intense red blossoms stand out even against its own green foliage (green and red being opposites.) That's one reason why Cardinal flower plants look so stunning when planted close together in large swaths. The greens and reds are amazingly intense and always draw the attention of Hummingbirds and humans!"

YEAR FIVE: 2014

A growing appreciation for native vines,
and even more biodiversity!

LEARNING ABOUT THE DIFFERENT NATIVE VINES IN OUR REGION

Native vines are some of the most fascinating of earth's gifts, if we think about the ways they have adapted to various environmental conditions over the eons, in order to survive. Mostly, as you can guess, vines have adapted to forest dwellings and they do everything they can to reach up to the sunlight. They twirl, they glue, they cling via aerial roots. Whatever it takes, vines will climb. We have had a lot of fun getting to know the "personality traits" of many of our Kentucky/Midwest native vines, including the following:

- Virgin's Bower (*Clematis virginica*)
- Dutchman's Pipevine (*Aristolochia macrophylla*)
- Leather Vase Vine (*Clematis viorna*)
- Coral Honeysuckle (*Lonicera sempervirens*)
- Carolina Milkvine (*Matelea carolinensis*)
- Passion Vine (*Passiflora*)
- Cross Vine (*Bignonia capreolata*)
- Virginia Creeper (*Parthenocissus quinquefolia*)
- Trumpet vine (*Campsis radicans*)

Virgin's Bower climbing into the branches of a dead tree, almost 25 feet above the ground, and a close-up of their blossoms.

Coral Honeysuckle, (*Lonicera sempervirens*), is a perfect replacement for the highly invasive Japanese honeysuckle (*Lonicera japonica*) that is invading our gardens and woodlands and crowding out native species. It is also a wonderful food source for hummingbirds and long-tongued bees. Trumpet Honeysuckle (*Campsis radicans*) pictured at the bottom of the page, is another ideal alternative to the invasive Japanese vine.

Native plants know what to do. With only a little help, Joe Pye Weed relocated to the dryer borders of the rain gardens; Cardinal Flower and Great Blue Lobelia formed a settlement at the water's edge, Monkey Flower, Eastern Blue Star, and Swamp Hibiscus migrated to the lowest points; while Seedbox, Butterfly Milkweed, and Jewel Weed cohabitated in the partly sunny, well-drained areas. Tall Tickseed, Autumn Sneezeweed, Bee Balm, Orange and Purple Coneflower willingly fill in available spaces as needed.

Monarchs and other butterflies flock to Joe Pye Weed blossoms in late summer. Fortunately, Joe Pye grows like a weed–in this case, a positive attribute.

Passiflora vine has spectacular blossoms. The fruit, the vines with their intricate twirling tendrils, and the foliage are also beautiful. Notice a couple of small bitemarks and some discoloration on the leaves–all perfectly normal since it's a host plant for the Gulf Fritillary. Below: Gulf Fritillary caterpillar, chrysalis, butterfly.

SWAMP HIBISCUS (HIBISCUS MOSCHEUTOS)

Bumblebees crawl inside swamp hibiscus blossoms for pollen, nectar, and to take naps—sometimes sleeping through the period when the blossom rolls back up for the night!

Below Left: Honeybees love Shrubby St. John's Wort and fill their back pockets with pollen. Below Right: Passion flower blossoms have "paddles" that apply pollen to the back of visiting bumblebees.

PURPLE CONEFLOWER (*ECHINACEA*)

Purple Coneflower develops eyelashes as the flower petals emerge from the buds.

A wink is as good as a nod when hinting at the blossom to come.

Below: Halberd Hibiscus, Jewel Weed, and Indigo Bush have developed their own specialized attributes.

PATHWAYS IN YOUR LANDSCAPE

Mulch pathways let the Earth breathe while minimizing unwanted grass, weeds, and mowing.

Stepping stones and a little grass allow for a nice blend of formality while promoting a good rapport with neighbors and housing associations!

Maidenhair Ferns form nice borders in shady areas. Large flagstones make great footbridges.

YEAR SIX: 2015

Signs of a Developing Ecosystem

MAGICAL MOMENTS

The leaves on Great Blue Lobelia begin vibrating before we spot the blur of a hummingbird whose wings are responsible for the downdraft. A clearwing moth hovers above beebalm and is always a welcome visitor.

EASTERN BLUESTAR (*AMSONIA TABERNAEMONTANA*)

Eastern Bluestar is an early bloomer with a profusion of delicate star-shaped blossoms that form a dome shape. The subtle foliage shelters rapier-thin seed pods that look like slender green beans and contain a milky, rubber-like substance that solidifies into seeds. It's also a survivor. (Pictured below)

(L) That is a mature Eastern Bluestar plant that has formed a clump against the side of a building. Despite the dry soil, and inattention, it is flourishing. That's Common Milkweed in the foreground. (Right) Another view of Eastern Bluestar and its foliage.

FINDING THE BEST PLACES TO THRIVE

(L Above) Grey-headed coneflower (taller) and orange coneflower in the foreground have migrated beyond the garden to the forest edge and don't require any babysitting. (R) Purple coneflower flourishing deeper within the same open woods. We didn't plant any of these. Native plants are independent! (Below L to R) Partridge Pea volunteers along the perimeter of our pathways, Cardinal Flower found a spot in the shade near the house, and a Swamp Milkweed plant moved to the forest.

EARLY SPRING BLOOMERS

Early spring ephemerals provide essential food for native bees that are just emerging from their winter slumber.

We started with three Mayapple (*Podophylum peltatum*) plants. Now we get two or three new ones (volunteers) each year. We're about out of fingers and toes when it comes time to count the recent additions, and the same is true for the neighboring sedges.

Foamflower (*Tiarella cordifolia*) and Wild Plum (*Prunus americana*)

(L) False Rue Anemone (Center) Shooting Star (R) Foam Flower

(L to R) Jack in the Pulpit, a catchy name for this unusual native plant. It's subtle, yet endearing, and a spring bloomer along with Dwarf Crested Iris and High Bush Vaccinium (Blueberry).

Despite the critical importance of early Spring flowers for our native pollinators, restoring them in our gardens is not as easy as one would think. Most retail nurseries are not up and running during the time of their emergence, so we must make an extra effort to find and plant bulbs, roots, and seeds in the Fall. Here is a summary of some of our current Spring ephemerals and early-blooming trees/shrubs native to Kentucky: Shooting Star, Spring Beauty, Mayapple, False Rue Anemone, Wild Ginger, Virginia Bluebells, Columbine, Dwarf-Crested Iris, American Plum Tree, Spicebush, Foam Flower, Harbinger of Spring, Jack in the Pulpit, and Wild Geranium.

THE ENDURANCE OF DROUGHT-TOLERANT NATIVE PLANTS

L - R: Despite drought, Tall Tickseed, Cardinal Flower, Orange Coneflower and Joe Pye Weed are determined to bloom.

In our area of Kentucky, we experience a lot of rain in the Spring, and then near-drought conditions in late Summer. Our native plant species are adapted to that cycle and, if the plants are in the right place for their needs, they can survive dry periods, as well as the flooded conditions of Spring. For example, the Pawpaw tree is most adapted to these conditions. From the moment the seed germinates, it begins to dig a deep taproot that will allow it to access water in late Summer. Being naturally caring people who want to nurture our plants, many of us tend to over-water native plants and trees in late Summer. If the leaves of your plantings show some stress during dry conditions, they may just be putting their energy into digging deeper for water. Over-watering causes plants to keep their roots closer to the surface, making them essentially weaker. Taller plants may fall over as well, because the shallow roots and weak stalks cannot bear the weight of the flowers and seed heads.

Indigo Bush is more like a small tree, with beautiful foliage and spectacular blossoms. The foliage is only on the top third of the shrub, so it can accommodate shorter plants and shrubs growing under it. It's also a host plant for many butterflies, including the California Gray Streak, whose caterpillar is pictured below. (Below right) Indigo bush blossom.

(Clockwise) Seedbox, Purple Coneflower, Swamp Hibiscus, Blue Flag Iris, Butterfly Milkweed, and Bee Balm. Aren't native wildflowers beautiful?

Left: Meadow Phlox, Middle: Monarch on Rose Milkweed, Right: Oxeye Sunflower

Planter boxes are also a nice way to mix and match native and non-native plants. Monarch Butterflies love Zinnias, but lay their eggs on Milkweed (Center,) because their caterpillars (Right) won't eat anything else!

Partridge Pea naturally enriches the soil, looks good doing it, and serves as a host plant for Cloudless Sulphur, Orange Sulphur, Gray Hairstreak, Sleepy Orange Butterflies, and Little Yellow caterpillars.

Creeping Phlox (*Phlox Stolonifera*) makes a wonderful groundcover. (Below clockwise) Wild Ginger, Heal All, and native ferns can serve as groundcover, too.

A trellis becomes a "squeeze-through" as native shrubs stretch for the sky, Orange Coneflower blooms where it's planted, Indigo Bush spreads its arms, and Coral Honeysuckle climbs along for the ride. They grow in harmony, and if you've ever seen Kudzu or exotic Wisteria smother their neighbors, you can appreciate the benefit of native plants.

2015 was the year that Orange Coneflower really took off. Over the years, this species adapted to both moist and dry soils and has formed its own small "islands" within the rain gardens. They look especially pretty mixed in with the complementary color of Great Blue Lobelia.

Seeds: Buried Treasure

(Clockwise): Seedbox seeds tend to rattle within the seed capsule; Echinacea; Blue Flag Iris; Butterfly Milkweed; Bee Balm; Swamp Hibiscus, and, Halberd Hibiscus seeds with a bonus blossom!

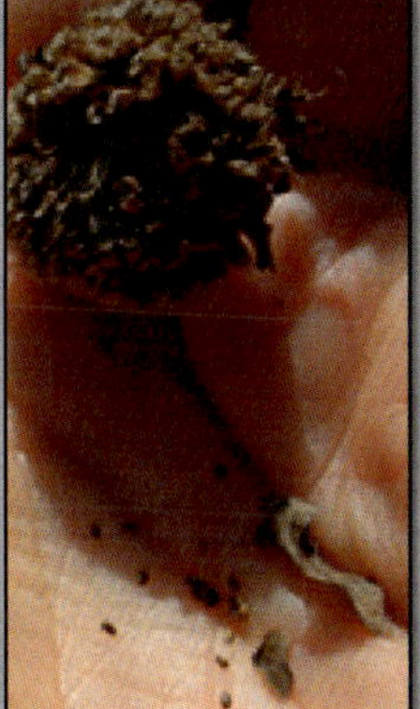

Researching the Back Story of Native Plants:

I, (Anne) absolutely love getting new native species. I enjoy researching the back stories of each and every one. And native plants, shrubs, trees and ferns DO have back stories on our continent and even in our more localized regions of the country. In the age of "googling," we can look up the traditional uses for many native plants as known to Native American tribes throughout history. Also, we can see how our ancestors used these native species for tea, coffee substitutes, nutritional food, wound care, etc. One year, after we had grown some Ninebark shrubs to maturity, I experimented with boiling the layers of shredding winter bark to obtain an orange dye that Native Americans used to deepen the shades of cedar wood. Also, I have created medicinal tonics from the blossoms and leaves of St. John's Wort and Chokeberry. Growing native plant species creates a personal sense of connection to our gardens that we can savor, each diverse species has its own personality, its own purpose, and its own caterpillars and other creatures that make use of it. This community of plants and pollinators share thousands of years of history together. They are adapted to each other and to the surrounding area. I feel strongly that, if we study the back story of a plant species, we will have more of an intuitive sense about where to plant them, and how to companion them with other native plants, shrubs, and trees.

Mother Nature gave these bees pockets on their legs to hold pollen. Mist Flower below, (R) Cut Leaf Prairie Dock

"Each of us has the ability to return to harmony with the web of life around us without becoming hermits or recluses or removing ourselves from our daily lives and society..."

Teri Uktena

Find us at:

www.LetTheEarthBreathe.org

ACTIVE PARTICIPANTS IN NATURAL CYCLES

No Need for Bird Feeders Anymore

For many years, nature lovers have enjoyed watching birds gather at their feeders, especially in winter when nothing else is happening. In our 12-year project, we have never used bird seed feeders. The reason is because the seeds in the feeders often do not come from the native species that we grow here and they are out of sync with the cycles that the birds have adapted to, over eons of time. We hope that people see the wisdom in planting a diversity of native species in this regard. Birds benefit from the seeds of native plants, and the caterpillars from many butterflies and moths depend on native species to survive; birds eat caterpillars in addition to seeds. It's all connected in seasonal cycles, unless we fill our yards with exotic plants. Elsewhere in this book, we have discussed how, every year now in July, the Goldfinches come when the native Echinacea and grey-head coneflowers go to seed. They feed their babies these seeds. Many of these seeds stay around all winter as birds naturally forage for food.

We leave the seed heads on the plants all winter because various caterpillars have already placed their winter chrysalises on or under these same plants. In the Spring (If they are not disturbed), the butterflies and moths emerge as the first cycle for that year. Those butterflies mate and make new versions of themselves, sometimes more than once in a season. Yes indeed, it's all connected. And it's truly healing and delightful to be an active participant in the way nature evolved long before we got here. We CAN participate!

When we create native plants sanctuaries, we are restoring, regenerating, and reinvigorating what is best and most "right" for the environment in which we live. We are not seeking to DOMINATE the natural world, but to participate in an entirely magical, self-sustaining ecosystem into which we humans fit perfectly, if we will only engage in a way that is cooperative rather than predatory.

The Swallowtail butterfly caterpillar attaches its rear end to a plant stem. It spins silk into a long thread, attaches it to the stem, and then wraps the thread around itself. Then it changes its outer shell to either brown or green, depending on what it is attached to. Now it's ready to hibernate until Spring. Amazing.

NATURAL BIRD SEED: NATIVE SUNFLOWERS

Maximillian Sunflowers

Steve: "Plant in poor soil and full sun, don't add water. With three plants this year, you'll have nine next year and thirty the year after that." I was selling native plants at the Farmer's Market.

"Sounds perfect." He was a teacher at nearby Moore High School.

To this day, a grove of Maximillian Sunflowers flourishes in a corner of the school's campus.

And the Earth breathes a little easier . . .

Below: Maximillian Sunflowers at our neighbor's house.

SEASONAL TRANSFORMATIONS

CORAL HONEYSUCKLE:
January and May

BLUE FLAG IRIS :
January and March

St. John's Wort:
January and June

SNOWBERRY leaf buds in January.
Leaves and new shoots in April,

YEARS 2016 AND ONWARD

Sharing the Abundance!

Early into our project, we grabbed the flat shovel and began cutting away the top layers of turf grass in one section of our front yard. This section was dry and sunny and soon became known to us as the "Prairie Garden." We did not amend the soil in this garden section at all because we planned to include only species that grew in the great tall grass prairies of the Midwest for eons before they were replaced by farming/agriculture. It has been really fun to watch many, many species of butterflies, moths, and skippers fly from flower to flower in our prairie garden and then watching the birds seek and find the seeds in the Fall and Winter. Here is a list of some of the most common species in our dry prairie garden area:

Purple Coneflower (*Echinacea*)
Bee Balm (*Monarda*)
Grey-headed Coneflower (*Ratibida pinnata*) -**(Photo)** →
Tall Ticseed (*Coreopsis tripteris*)
Hairy Mountain Mint (*Pycnanthemum verticillatum*)
Orange Butterfly Milkweed (*Asclepias tuberosa*)
Cut-leaf Prairie Dock (*Silphium pinnatifidum*)
Maximillian's Sunflower (*Helianthus maximiliani*)
Orange Coneflower (*Rudbeckia fulgida*)
New England Asters (*Symphyotrichum novae-angliae*)
Smooth Penstemon (*Penstemon digitalis*)
Partridge Pea (*Chamaecrista fasciculata*)
Dense Blazing Star (*Liatris Spicata*)
Ironweed (*Vernonia missurica*)

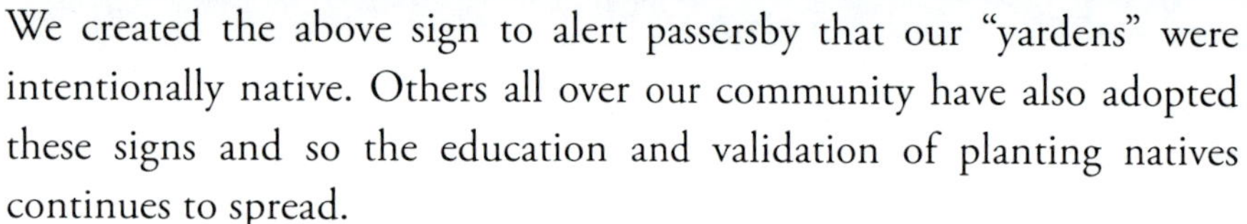
We created the above sign to alert passersby that our "yardens" were intentionally native. Others all over our community have also adopted these signs and so the education and validation of planting natives continues to spread.

EXPANSION THROUGH SHARING AND EDUCATION IN SCHOOLS

Steve: From 2016-2018, I managed a grant to enhance school urban garden initiatives with Kentucky native plants, shrubs, and trees. Now the earth can breathe a little easier in 53 more locations here in Louisville, Kentucky. The program helped students learn and apply math, science, technology, and engineering skills by installing native plant gardens. Most of the schools have been good stewards and their native plant gardens have expanded at the school, at students' homes, and into the surrounding neighborhoods. Sister schools that weren't part of the initial program were inspired and installed native plant gardens. According to many of the teachers, the best way to get students to behave is to promise them time in the garden! The students have learned how much fun it is to put plants in the ground and have witnessed how pollinators benefit from native plant species. When pollinators benefit; we ALL benefit. (Swamp Milkweed and a visitor at Assumption High School. 2nd row L to R: installing gardens at Kennedy and Englehardt Elementary Schools.

A PEACE GARDEN

People are pollinators, too. The students at St. Francis of Assisi Catholic School had planted a pollinator garden the previous year, so they scheduled a cultural field trip to The Islamic School of Louisville to help their students establish a new garden. The St. Francis students prepared for their trip by learning how to greet their new friends in Arabic. After the planting, the Islamic School students provided lunch as a way of showing their appreciation. It was a beautiful event and a positive step toward tolerance and mutual understanding.

Below: One of my favorite "before and after "pictures.

EXPANDING INTO NATIVE PLANT AND SEED SWAPS

Geographically, Kentucky is an extraordinarily diverse area that can accommodate native species that are adapted to north, south, east, and west climates. Therefore, once we reached the place where we had more than 60 thriving native plant species, we began to run out of room! That's when the idea came to us to begin sharing seeds and plants. Our first native plants swap was held in 2019 and we had a few early adapters attend. We are still enjoying the plants we have been growing from seeds we obtained at that first swap. Now, however, our Facebook page has over 1000 members from the greater Louisville area and we have split our larger group into mini-swaps according to Louisville neighborhoods. The "socially-distanced" 1:1 plant swaps that took place during the Covid-19 pandemic provided great support to many people who were lonely and isolated during that time. Through our expanding neighborhood swaps, we have begun forming communities of home, school, and church gardens that provide healthy connections for individuals and large swaths of native plants for our pollinators.

The Let the Earth Breathe Foundation, Inc.

In 2021, after years of observing the heartbreaking removal (by developers) of hundreds of thousands of acres of open space around our area, we decided to respond by creating a non-profit foundation to fund projects that save open space and create larger swaths of native plants, shrubs and trees.

If you'd like to learn more, and donate to our work, please visit our website at www.Lettheearthbreathe.org

IN CLOSING (FOR NOW) SEPTEMBER, 2021

On one of the last days before the release of this book I (Anne) was standing beside a patch of Swamp Milkweed, the seedpods of which had just cracked open. I was reflecting on how far we'd come over the 12 years of this very special project. A slight breeze came up from the north, sending the feather-like Milkweed seeds southward as if floating on clouds of invisible light. A Monarch Butterfly rose up from the patch and joined the floating seeds, perhaps ready to begin the next phase of its own migration journey south. I couldn't help but be delighted with the scene, and I felt a kind of confirmation that what we've done is a good thing, and for a greater good than just ourselves. Like the butterfly and the seeds, we let it all go, with the blessing of angels and fairies, and look forward to seeing what happens next as each of us contributes something wonderful to the pollinators and to our planet. Thank you for letting us share our journey with you. Happy Planting!

Steve: I have developed a peaceful and meditative morning ritual of "Zen weeding." I drink some coffee and pull some weeds, or simply admire the evolving nature of our project. Fortunately, most native plants outgrow the weeds. I have noticed the simple beauty of native plant blossoms and grown to admire their hardiness. I never knew there were so many bugs! Our garden is full of "stealth bugs" that have been sharing our garden space, and it is only when I slow my mind that I notice their remarkable variety and incredible coloration. The complexity and originality of each plant is a four-season delight. Jewelweed seed pods burst open when touched and send their seeds flying. There is a marvelous metamorphosis when ferns unfurl their fronds in spring. It's like greeting old friends when Joe Pye Weed blooms, familiar and welcome. I'm amazed at how fast these plants grow, how soon they blossom and for how long, and how they gracefully make way for the next round of neighboring plants in the ebb and flow of blooming cycles. And next year it will continue . . . there is always something new to discover, rediscover, or simply appreciate.

APPENDIX/PLANT LIST

RESOURCES

Pollinator resources online

Native Plant Finder: https://www.nwf.org/NativePlantFinder

USDA Plant database: https://plants.sc.egov.usda.gov/home

Pollinator Partnership: www.pollinator.org

North American Pollinator Protection Campaign: www.nappc.org

Attracting Pollinators to Your Garden. fws.gov/pollinators/

Recommended Books

Bringing Nature Home. Douglas W. Tallamy

Nature's Best Hope: A New Approach to Conservation That Starts in Your Yard. Douglas W. Tallamy

Wildflowers and Ferns of Kentucky. Thomas Barnes

Native Plants of the Midwest: A Comprehensive Guide to the Best 500 Species for the Garden. Alan Branhagen

Where to find native plants

Dropseed Nursery: www.dropseednursery.com (Goshen, KY)

Bean Native Nursery and Consulting: beannativenursery.com (Cincinnati, OH)

Roundstone Native Seed Company: roundstoneseed.com (Kentucky)

Grow Wilder Native Plant Nursery (Pioneer Village, in Bullitt County, KY)

ReSeed Native Plant Nursery (New Albany, IN)

Kentucky Native Plant Society https://www.knps.org/native-plant-nurseries/

Indiana Native Plant Society: https://indiananativeplants.org/landscaping/where-to-buy/

Tennessee Native Plant Society: https://www.tnps.org/

Midwest Native Plant Society: https://www.midwestnativeplants.org/

Kentucky Division of Forestry-State Nurseries and Tree seedlings

United States Department of Agriculture: https://plants.sc.egov.usda.gov/java/

Gulf Fritillary photo: USDA, Photo by Beatriz Moisset

Gulf Fritillary caterpillar and chrysalis: http://lepcurious.blogspot.com/2015/07/gulf-fritillary.html

Plant	Full Sun	Shade	Part Sun & Shade	Bloom Time	Blossom Color	Height	Additional Information
ALLEGHENY SPURGE (*PACHYSANDRA PROCUMBENS*)		X	X	March to April	White	6-12 inches.	Makes a nice ground cover.
AMERICAN HOLLY (*ILEX OPACA*)	X		X	May	Creamy White	15-30 ft.	A broadleaf evergreen.
AMERICAN SENNA (SENNA HEBECARPA)	X		X	Late Summer	Yellow	4-5 ft.	Attracts butterflies and other pollinators, and has pretty fall foliage. Restores the soil.
AQUATIC MILKWEED (ASCLEPIAS PERENNIS)	X			July - August	White, pink, mauve	4-5 ft.	Showy flowers attract butterflies and pollinators.
AUTUMN SNEEZEWEED (*HELENIUM AUTUMNALE*)			X	Late summer	Yellow	1-3 ft.	Doesn't cause hay fever: the pollen grains are too big. A late bloomer when most colors are fading.
BEEBALM (*MONARDA FISTULOSA*)	X		X	Mid-summer	Light Blue	4-5 ft.	Great for attracting bumblebees, hummingbirds, and butterflies. Comes back strong, spreads very well.
BIG BLUESTEM (*ANDROPOGON GERADII*)	X		X	Mid-late summer	Green	3-9 ft.	Tall, native grass. Does better in full sun, will tolerate partial sun/ shade. Great at stabilizing areas and anchoring drainages. Pretty fall foliage.
BLACK CHOKEBERRY (*ARONIA MELANOCARPA*)			X	Early	Green leaves white blossoms	3-5 ft.	Adaptable shrub that suckers freely. An early bloomer with pretty fall foliage.
BLACK-EYED SUSAN (*RUDBECKIA HIRTA*)	X		X	Mid-summer	Orange with black centers	2-3 ft.	Prefers full sun but will bloom in partial shade.
BLAZING STAR (*LIATRIS SPICATA*)	X			July-August	Purple stalks	2-4 ft.	Showy flowers attract birds and butterflies.

Plant	Full Sun	Shade	Part Sun & Shade	Bloom Time	Blossom Color	Height	Additional Information
BLUE VERVAIN (*VERBENA HASTATA*)	X			Mid-summer		4-5 ft.	Delicate, light-blue or purple flowers, prefers moist soil, and does better in full sun but willing to accept a little shade.
COMMON MILKWEED (*ASCLEPIAS SYRIACA*)	X			Mid-summer	White/Pink blossoms	4-6 ft.	Waxy green leaves. The best for attracting monarchs and once established is a survivor.
CORALBERRY (*SYMPHORICARPOS ORBICULATUS*)	X		X	June - July	Pinkish-white	4-8 ft.	Forms colonies by suckering, the berries are a good source of food for birds
CREEPING PHLOX (*PHLOX STOLONIFERA*)			X	Early	Bluish-purple flowers	6-10 inches	Great along borders or in planting boxes. Works as a ground cover with the added bonus of having flowers.
CROSSVINE (*BIGNONIA CAPREOLATA*)			X	Mid-spring to late summer	Orange w/ yellow insides	Vine	Tubular flowers that attract hummingbirds and butterflies. Great for fences and trellises.
CULVERS ROOT (*VERONICASTRUM VIRGINICUM*)	X		X	Summer	White	2-5 ft.	Densely packed spikes of tiny white flowers. Adds height to a garden.
CUT LEAF PRAIRIE DOCK (*SILPHIUM PINNATIFIDUM*)	X		X	Mid to Late summer	Yellow blossoms	6-10 ft.	Big basal leaves producing tall stalks with multiple blossoms. Attracts a wide variety of insects.
DENSE BLAZING STAR (*LIATRIS SPICATA*)			X	Mid-summer	Spiked blue to purple blossoms	4-5 ft.	Honeybees and bumblebees love this.

Plant	Full Sun	Shade	Part Sun & Shade	Bloom Time	Blossom Color	Height	Additional Information
EASTERN BLUESTAR (*AMSONIA TABERNAEMONTANA*)		X	X	Early	Delicate blue star-shaped blossoms	2-4 ft.	Grows in clumps and likes moist soil. The blossoms and seed pods are especially attractive.
EASTERN REDBUD (*CERCIS CANADENSIS*)	X		X	April	Showy and pink	25-30 ft	Beautiful blossoms that are edible and taste like cabbage. Attracts butterflies.
EASTERN WAHOO (*EUONYMUS ATROPURPUREUS*)	X		X	June	Purple	15-25 ft.	Attractive red berries and pretty fall color.
ELDERBERRY (*SAMBUCUS CANADENSIS*)			X	Early	White blossoms and purple berries	5-12 ft.	Easy to transplant. Fast-growing understory bush that can form hedges.
FLOWERING DOGWOOD TREES (*CORNUS FLORIDA*)			X	Early	White blossoms	5-30 ft.	Attracts birds and butterflies, pretty foliage with early blossoms.
FOAM FLOWER (*TIARELLA CORDIFOLIA*)		X		Early	Spikes of white blossoms	6"-1 ft.	Does well in shade. An early bloomer and a welcome sight in spring to the impatient gardener.
FOX SEDGE (*CAREX VULPINOIDEA*)			X		Hardy sedge	6-18"	Seed clusters on slender stalks look like fox-tails. Spreads well and is a personal favorite because it's a survivor.
FRANK'S SEDGE (*CAREX FRANKII*)			X		Broad green leaves	1-3 ft.	Spreads and does well in wet or moist soil, yet drought tolerant. A survivor and the seed pods are attractive.

Plant	Full Sun	Shade	Part Sun & Shade	Bloom Time	Blossom Color	Height	Additional Information
GOLD STONECROP (*SEDUM SARMENTOSUM*)			X	X	white	2-6 inches	An early bloomer and a nice ground cover that spreads fast but isn't aggressive, fades in direct sun but comes back every year. Easy to transplant.
GRAY-HEADED CONEFLOWER (*RATIBIDA PINNATA*)	X		X		Yellow petals/ gray center	3-5 ft.	Grows in clumps and spreads easily. Doesn't require much care and the blossom centers turn from gray to dark brown as it matures.
GREAT BLUE LOBELIA (*LOBELIA SIPHILITICA*)		X	X	Mid to late summer	Multiple blue blossoms on spikes	1-3 ft.	Great for attracting hummingbirds and specialty bees. The florets stay green all year.
HONEYVINE MILKWEED (*CYNANCHUM LAEVE*)	X		X	July - September	White clusters	Vine up to 13 ft.	The blossoms smell like honey. Great for disturbed soil.
HALBERDLEAF ROSEMALLOW (*HIBISCUS LAEVIS*)	X		X		White with pink centers	4-6 ft.	Produces large, beautiful blossoms during Summer and into Fall. A favorite for butterflies, bumblebees, and other native pollinators.
ILLINOIS BUNDLEFLOWER (*DESMANTHUS ILLINOENSIS*)	X		X	Mid to late summer	Small white blossoms	1-3 ft.	Fluffy white flowers with beautiful frond-like leaves that curl up at night, produces attractive seed pods in an array of graceful curves.

Plant	Full Sun	Shade	Part Sun & Shade	Bloom Time	Blossom Color	Height	Additional Information
INDIGO BUSH (*AMORPHA FRUITICOSA*)	X		X	Spring	Purple and golden spikes	6-10 ft.	Spectacular blossoms. Graceful leaves. Ideal as a perimeter shrub/tree.
IRONWEED (*VERNONIA GIGANTEA*)	X		X	Mid to late Summer	Purple	4-6 ft.	Prefers full sun, but will grow in part shade. Adds welcome color later in Fall.
MAYAPPLE (*PODOPHYLUM PELTATUM*)		X		Spring	White with yellow centers	8″ to 18″	One of the first plants to appear in Spring. Leaves form green umbrellas. Spreads and colonizes shady areas before the trees leaf out.
MIST FLOWER (*CONOCLINUIM COELESTINUM*)	X		X	Summer	Pale blue clusters	1-3 ft.	Will bloom in shade/part sun. Spreads well and is a favorite with specialty bees. Thrives beneath shrubs and lends a welcome burst of color to shady areas.
MONKEY FLOWER (*MIMULUS RINGENS*)			X	Summer	Blue	1-4 ft.	Grows along drainages and pond areas. A survivor that hangs on despite flooding and swift runoff.
NEW ENGLAND ASTER *ASTER NOVAE-ANGLIAE*	X		X	Mid to late Summer to Fall	Deep purple to pink petals with yellow centers	1-2 ft.	Large, dynamic blossoms that add welcome color in late summer and into fall. Does better in full sun
NORTHERN RED OAK (*QUERCUS RUBRA*)	X				Yellowish-green	50 - 75 ft.	Fast-growing with beautiful foliage.

Plant	Full Sun	Shade	Part Sun & Shade	Bloom Time	Blossom Color	Height	Additional Information
OBEDIENT PLANT (*PHYSOSTEGIA VIRGINIANA*)	X		X	June - September	Pink to White	3-4 feet	Showy stalks of bell-shaped flowers, blooms from bottom to top.
ORANGE CONEFLOWER (*RUDBECKIA FULGIDA*)	X		X	Summer	Orange to yellow with black centers	2-3 ft.	A willing survivor, blooms where planted. Spreads easily and comes back strong—perfect for the black-thumbed gardener.
PARTRIDGE PEA (*CHAMAECRISTA FASCICULATA*)		X	X	Summer	Yellow with red centers	1-3 ft.	Naturally adds nitrogen to the soil (good!) A bumblebee magnet. Frond-like leaves and attractive seed pods. Reseeds.
PASSIONFLOWER (*PASSIFLORA INCARNATA*)			X	Summer	Pale purple flowers with decorative white centers	Vine 3-15 ft pr. season	Aggressive, fast-growing vine producing beautiful flowers, dark green leaves, and fruit similar to a small green pomegranate. Adaptable, but a little aggressive and may need to be thinned or pulled up.
PAWPAW TREES (*ASIMINA TRILOBA*)			X	Spring	Brownish-red that smell bad to attract flies!	May reach 25 ft.	Endearing understory tree with delicious fruit that tastes like a cross between a mango and a banana. You'll need two or more for cross-pollination.
RED BUCKEYE (*AESCULUS PAVIA*)	X		X	April-May	Bright Red	12-15 ft.	Attracts hummingbirds, showy fruit and blossoms.

Plant	Full Sun	Shade	Part Sun & Shade	Bloom Time	Blossom Color	Height	Additional Information
RED CHOKEBERRY (*ARONIA ARBUTIFOLIA*)			X	April	White	6-12 ft.	Showy red fruit that lasts into winter.
RED-TWIG DOGWOOD (*CORNUS SERICEA*)	X		X	May-June	White, showy flowers	6-9 ft.	Attracts birds and butterflies, tolerates a wide range of soils.
RIVER CANE (*ARUNDINARIA GIGANTEA*)	X			Rarely flowers		5-12 ft.	Friendly alternative to bamboo. Prefers moist soil.
ROYAL CATCHFLY (*SILENE REGIA*)	X			Summer	Red	2-5 ft.	Pretty, scarlet-red flowers great for attracting butterflies.
ROYAL FERN (*OSMUNDA REGALIS*)		X				Up to 6 ft.	Delightful to watch the fronds unfurl–a positive indicator of Spring. Comes back bigger and stronger every year.
SUNDROPS (*OENOTHERA FRUTICOSE*)	X			May - June	Yellow	1-1.5 ft.	Prefers full sun, can tolerate some shade.
SWAMP HIBISCUS (*HIBISCUS MOSCHEUTOS*)		X	X	Summer	Large pink flowers	4-5 ft.	Produces a profusion of large, dramatic blossoms, prefers wet to moist soil.
SWAMP MILKWEED (*ASCLEPIAS INCARNATA*)	X		X	Summer	Pinkish-red clusters	5 ft.	Prefers full sun and moist to wet soil. May need to be replanted yearly, but a butterfly magnet with gorgeous flowers.
SWITCHGRASS (*PANICUM VIRGATUM*)	X					3-6 ft.	Forms clumps–ideal for drainages, leaves turn yellow-orange for Fall colors; showy seed heads are a great food source for animals.

Plant	Full Sun	Shade	Part Sun & Shade	Bloom Time	Blossom Color	Height	Additional Information
TALL TICKSEED (*COREOPSIS TRIPTERIS*)	X		X	Summer	Yellow	4-7 ft.	A survivor, does better in sun, will grow in part sun/ shade, forms colonies, spreads, with attractive mid to late season yellow blossoms.
TRUMPET HONEYSUCKLE (*LONICERA SEMPERVIRENS*)			X	Spring Summer Fall	Orange-red-yellow	Vine	Hummingbird magnet. Beautiful leaves and trumpet-shaped blossom clusters. A "must-have" that comes back stronger and thicker every year.
VIBURNUM (*Viburnum Dentatum*)	X		X	Spring	White	5-10 ft.	Important host plant for caterpillars, moths, and butterflies.
VIRGINIA SWEETSPIRE (*ITEA VIRGINICA*)	X		X	May to June	White, fragrant, drooping cylinders.	3-4 ft.	Red, orange, and gold fall foliage.
VIRGIN'S BOWER (*CLEMATIS VIRGINIANA*)		X	X	Fall	White	Vine	Fast-growing, late-blooming vine that grows well in shade. Pretty white blossoms. A little aggressive, but easy to cull.
WILD GERANIUM (*GERANIUM MACULATUM*)		X		Spring	Purple	1-2 ft.	Prefers moist soil. An early bloomer and pretty spring wildflower that will put a smile on your face. The more you look at it, the prettier you realize it is!
WILD GINGER (*ASARUM CANADENSE*)		X		Early Spring	Purplish-brown	6-12 inches	Makes a great groundcover.

Plant	Full Sun	Shade	Part Sun & Shade	Bloom Time	Blossom Color	Height	Additional Information
WILD LUPINE (*LUPINUS PERENNIS*)		X		Spring	Blue	8 in. to 2 ft.	Stalks of pretty, light-blue flowers. Fast germinating if you scar (scrape) the outer seed coat. Attracts the Karner Blue Butterfly—spectacular to watch but nearly extinct.
WILD PHLOX (*PHLOX DIVARICATA*)		X		Spring	Lavender	1 ft.	Thrives in poor soil and grows well in shade. Can be used as a ground cover. Beautiful star-shaped blossoms.
WILD PLUM (*PRUNUS AMERICANA*)	X		X	Spring	White	10-24 ft.	Beautiful blossoms and forms a canopy as wide as it is tall.
WINTERBERRY HOLLY (*ILEX VERTICILLATA*)	X		X	June-July	Greenish-white	3-12 ft.	Great at attracting birds. Low maintenance. Makes a nice hedge
WOOD POPPY (*STYLOPHORUM DIPHYLLUM*)		X		Spring	Yellow	1 ft.	An early bloomer with bright blossoms and pretty, long-lasting foliage.

Black chokeberry (*Aronia melanocarpa*) blossom in early Spring.

INDEX

Made in United States
North Haven, CT
03 December 2021